Betta Splendens for Beginners

Species Appropriate Care for a Fighting Fish

ALINA DARIA

ISBN: 9798713069056

Contents

What Are Betta Fish?

The scientific name of the most popular fighting fish is *Betta splendens*, although there are more than sixty different types of fighting fish. They are often also called labyrinth fish, betta fish or simply bettas. The name *betta* comes from the Javanese language and was derived from the terms *wader bettah* and *ikan bettah* (ikan = fish). This is said to mean *biting fish*. Due to consistency and uniformity, we will use the term *betta fish* in the following.

Betta fish belong to the labyrinth fish because they have the so-called labyrinth organ. With the help of this organ, they absorb atmospheric oxygen and can therefore live in warm water. The warmer a specific water is, the less oxygen there is in the water. Due to their labyrinth organ, betta fish are therefore not only dependent on their gill breathing, but also take in air at the water surface with their mouth. They belong to the small freshwater fishes and are part of the osphronemidae family.

© *StockSnap*

Betta fish are native to Cambodia, Indonesia, Bali, Myanmar and Thailand, among other places - thus in Southeast Asia. For many years, however, betta fish have also been popular pets in home tanks. Our domesticated betta fish come mainly from Cambodia and Thailand. In the wild in Asia, the wild forms live in streams, rivers and canals as well as in ponds and lakes.

Around 1890, the betta fish also found its way to Europe. However, this fish species has been bred for many centuries.

Betta fish usually grow to a size of about five to seven centimetres and live for about two to four years if they are kept in a species-appropriate manner. However, there are also so-called giants that grow even larger.

Betta fish in the breeding form are strict loners - socialising with other betta fish or other fish species can lead to fights that can result in mutilation and death of the inferior fish. Furthermore, general stress should be avoided, as stress can also shorten the life expectancy - sometimes drastically. Good water values, a suitable water temperature and sufficient plants are very important.

Betta fish can be roughly divided into the wild types and the breeding types. The wild forms usually come in various shades of brown and red, while the breeding forms can nowadays be found in many different colours.

The fins of the wild types are relatively short and flag-like, while the fins of the breaded forms can often be very long - and in some cases even larger than the fish body itself.

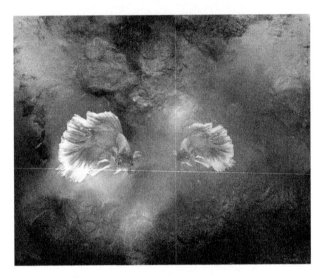

© Renate Anna Becker

Wild Type

The wild types of the betta fish live in waters with little or no current. These waters are usually shallow, and they can even be found in rice fields and the like. Since they also breathe atmospheric oxygen, betta fish rarely stay in deep waters.

The males have longer fins than the females and usually have a stronger, more distinct colouration. Females have shorter fins, and their colours are usually paler.

The wild type is not as aggressive as the breaded types but should preferably also be kept in solitary confinement. They do not live in groups in the wild, but usually only come together to breed and then go their separate ways again. They are also territorial and do not like it when someone else invades their territory.

The males are usually more aggressive than the females. Fights between male betta fish often end with the death of the inferior animal. In females, it happens that they tolerate each other once they have established a hierarchy. But even this is not always the case. In order to avoid disputes and fights, it is advisable to keep the animals in single-household conditions.

© *Sirawit Seengam*

Breeding Type

Betta Splendens

The breaded types of betta fish are even more aggressive than the wild types. While keeping the wild types in groups may work, but only occasionally - for example, if a male is kept with two females (harem keeping) or if two to three females live together - this is strictly to be avoided for betta splendens. No distinction should be made between males and females; both belong in single housing. Both males and females usually fight each other until the death of the inferior fish.

Betta splendens fish also form their territory and defend it. They were bred specifically for competition; their aggressiveness was thus desired by the breeders! They were put together for fights and people bet on which fish would win the fight. For this purpose, the fish were let loose on each other in a small vessel, often holding only two to seven litres of water. In most cases, a fight lasted until one of the animals died. The animals had robust, strong bodies and short fins. The breeding of long-finned bettas took place somewhat later.

Accordingly, high-breeds do not occur in the wild and have their "home" with breeders and pet lovers. In pet shops, too, you will find almost exclusively high-breeds. The wild types are usually not offered and often have to be imported if necessary.

Betta fish are available in many different colours and with many different fin shapes. Breeding is done according to the standards of the IBC (*International Betta Congress*) and exhibitions of particularly magnificent specimens are often held.

The betta fish should also not be kept together with other fish species. For example, there are fish that like to nibble at the betta fish's beautiful fins and thus injure the betta fish. In addition, other fish in the betta fish's territory cause great stress. The betta fish is used to having its territory to itself and not wanting or having to share it. However, it usually has no problem with snails or shrimps as co-inhabitants.

If a betta fish has to live in a community tank with other fish, it usually starts by defending its territory and claiming it for itself. Even if the other fish want to leave the territory, they cannot do so because they are logically "trapped" in the tank together with the betta fish. So, there is no way to get out of each other's way. The fish start attacking each other and tearing and nibbling at each other's fins.

The betta fish now slowly loses its strength and, in most cases, eventually gives up trying to defend its territory. It comes to terms with the situation but is not happy with it and instead becomes extremely stressed as it is "robbed" of its territory. Therefore, it is not uncommon for betta fish in community tanks to live only a few weeks or only a few months, while they can live up to three or four years in single keeping.

The longer and larger the fins of a betta fish, the less it usually swims. Therefore, betta fish with pronounced fins need less space than short-finned fish. In animal husbandry, one usually speaks of minimum dimensions that the home of a respective animal should have, and there are often no upper limits.

This is different with the betta fish. The larger the betta fish's fins are, the less it usually swims. In addition, betta fish often feel more comfortable when they have a good view of their territory. Therefore, a tank that "only" holds 25 to 30 litres is sufficient for most betta fish. This way they have a good overview of their territory. Tanks that are too large can even stress some betta fish.

One might assume that betta fish with larger fins have to swim more than betta fish with shorter fins. In

BETTA SPLENDENS FOR BEGINNERS

reality, however, this is not the case. Short-finned betta fish are usually more active and move around more than long-finned betta fish. However, even with long-finned fish, care should be taken that the fins do not "atrophy" but are used often. A good way to do this is, for example, mirror or pen training.

A mirror is held up to the betta fish. It then starts to spread its fins and trains them so that they do not atrophy. In pen training, a pen is slowly moved back and forth in front of the tank. The betta fish "chases" the pen and thereby trains its fins as well. Such training can be done about once a week. It is not compulsory, but it is especially useful for long-finned fish to keep their fins active.

© Sirawit Seengam

Types and Colours of the Betta Splendens

The breeding standards are mainly set by the internationally active IBC (*International Betta Congress*), which most breeders follow. The IBC organises over forty betta fish shows per year worldwide, making it the largest organisation. As this is a book for beginners, not all breeding forms are presented, as there are now already more than sixty different ones.

Over the years, many different colours and fin types have been bred. The first fin type bred was the Veil Tail, so called because it resembles a bridal veil.

One can roughly distinguish between three fin types. These are the Long Tail, the Short Tail and the

Double Tail. However, each of these types of fins comes in many different forms.

The long-finned species includes the aforementioned veil tail, which is reminiscent of a bridal veil. Veil tails look very grandiose and are therefore very popular in the home tank.

The so-called Super Delta is able to spread its fins very wide and even reach 180°.

The Half Moon spreads its fins even further and reaches even more than the previously mentioned 180°.

The Crown Tail belongs to the Round Tails and its fin rays are pointed. Depending on the number of individual fin rays, this can be further separated.

The fins of the Spade Tail look like a brush, but this fin shape is no longer as common as, for example, the Veil Tail, the Half Moon or the Crown Tail.

The short-finned species include the "normal" plakat, the half-moon plakat with a fin span of 180° and the traditional plakat, which can also spread its fins to 180° but has a bifurcation in the fin rays.

The Double Tail has a double fin tail, but there are also special forms here in combination with the Short Fin - for example, there is the Double Tail Plakat, which has a double tail fin, but it is very short.

Regarding the colours, it is first important to know that betta fish have different layers. These are not always visible and together result in the colouration of the fish. The layer order of the wild types is different from the layer order of the betta splendens.

The layers in both wild and breaded forms consist of the yellow layer, the black layer, the red layer and the uppermost layer, the so-called main layer, which shimmers on the surface of the body. The yellow layer is the lowest layer in all betta fish. In wild forms, this is followed by the black layer, then the red layer and finally the main layer. The black and red layers are "swapped" in the breaded forms - the yellow layer is followed by the red layer, then the black layer and then the main layer. The top layer is called the iridescent top layer.

A betta fish thus has four colour layers. These layers each have a genetic code, which together determine the colouration of the fish as a whole. The genetic codes either reduce or increase the pigment intensity. Let's take a closer look at the 20 most common colours:

1. Black Lace: The black lace is black, but also has blue tones. This is not the case with the Melano Black (see below).

2. Butterfly: The butterfly can be found in different colours, but has an even, light outline on the edge of the body. In some cases, the outline is also black, but mostly white.

3. Cambodian: The cambodian has a light body and mostly blue or red fin colours.

4. Chocolate: It will come as no surprise that the chocolate is brown. While the body can be various shades of brown, the fins are usually yellowish.

5. Cello: Cello stands for cellophane. A cello is blue or green and its fins appear slightly translucent.

6. Copper: In the copper, the betta splendens has been crossed with the betta mahachai or betta imbellis. The copper comes in many different colour forms, but the proportion of opaque genes is very high. Coppers have a kind of "metallic" sheen.

7. Dragon: The dragon has a very thick cover layer, thicker than its conspecifics. The older the fish gets, the thicker the top layer usually becomes. However, it should be noted that this breeding form can cause or increase the risk of diseases such as blindness or

tumours. Like the copper, the dragon has a metallic sheen.

8. Galaxy: The galaxy comes in different colour varieties, but they all have glossy scales, which are mostly black or white speckled.

9. Gold: Not surprisingly, this is a golden betta fish.

10. Lavender: Lavenders have a pale body, but their fins are bluish. The edge of the fins is red or light red.

11. Mamba: A mamba is black in colour but has some glossy scales with a white tinge.

12. Marble: Marbles were discovered or bred rather by chance. They exist in all colour varieties and they change their colour. A marble can even change its colour from white to black, for example, and often these changes continue until the end of its life.

Actually, the prison inmate Orville Gulley only wanted to breed black butterflies in his captivity, but in the process, he came across the marble gene. How the colours change in the course of the fish's life is difficult or impossible to control.

13. Melano black: A melano black is black throughout.

14. Mustard: The mustard originally had a bluish/greenish body and blue/yellow fins. Nowadays, however, it is also found in other colour combinations, some of which are darker.

15. Opaque: Opaque betta fish are either green or blue. The blue is again differentiated into steel blue and royal blue. However, they are covered by a whitish layer, which looks like a "powder layer".

16. Pastel: The pastel also comes in green and blue. Here, too, a distinction is made between Steel Blue and Royal Blue. However, the pastel is not covered by a whitish, powdery layer.

17. Pineapple: A pineapple is dark yellow and slightly brownish.

18. Platinum: A platinum resembles a pastel, but the platinum is more shimmery and shinier.

19. Salamander: A salamander is red or pink; the colour often appears slightly purple. The edges of its fins are white.

20. Iridescent colours: The so-called iridescent colours include steel blue, royal blue and turquoise.

© *Sirawit Seengam*

Purchasing the Betta Fish

For many people, the pet shop is the first place to go when buying a pet. In most pet shops, you will find what you are looking for if you are looking for betta fish, because they are very popular fish, especially because of their beauty. However, it should be borne in mind that pet shops often regard the animals as mere products, have them "produced" en masse and often do not attach much importance to proper breeding and keeping conditions. Furthermore, pet shops still often give wrong advice - for example, it is not uncommon to be advised to keep them in groups or even to keep them together with other fish species.

Therefore, it is usually better to turn to breeders with years of experience in breeding betta fish. You can recognise a serious breeder by the fact that he/she keeps the fish in a species-appropriate manner, can trace the pedigrees and explains everything important to the beginner. There are also many breeders who ship their fish. If this is well prepared and done as stress-free as possible, shipping animals is no problem.

Some owners have special types of betta fish - especially wild types - delivered from the respective home countries and the fish travel from Indonesia, Malaysia etc. to the destination country. I personally advise against this. In Asian countries betta fish are usually not kept well. They often live in bowls, tubs, bottles or similar. Costs are kept as low as possible, even if this is detrimental to animal welfare. Unfortunately, it often happens that imported betta fish are already sick and introduce parasites, for example. Such long transport routes are of course also very stressful for a fish!

Breeders in western countries, especially in Europe, usually keep betta fish as a hobby and make little or no profit. More value is usually placed on a species-appropriate life and the animals are better cared for. Transport distances are shorter and therefore more pleasant for the fish. Therefore, I advise you to buy betta fish from a breeder in the same country where you live.

Most betta fish are ready for release at about five months and can move into a new home. However, they are not fully grown until they are about six to eight months old.

It is quite normal for breeders to charge a small fee to cover their costs and to be sure that the buyer is serious about keeping betta fish. However, this fee should also not be too high. A price between ten and forty GBP (15 to 50 US dollars) is normal and appropriate.

© *Sirawit Seengam*

Home

Since betta fish in the breeding form are strict loners and - as the name *fighting fish* already suggests - fight with other betta fish as well as sometimes with other fish species, each betta fish should have its own tank. This should be at least a 25-litre tank. Usually, tanks with a volume of 30 to 50 litres are recommended; this is fine. Betta fish with short fins tend to need a little more space than betta fish with large, long fins.

If you do want to keep several betta fish together, this is only possible with the wild types of betta fish. Betta splendens - i.e., the breeding forms - should always be kept alone. Wild forms that can live together include betta smaragdina, betta simplex or betta imbellis.

As betta fish are known to "like" to jump out of the water, the tank should have a lid. This also protects the fish from other possible pets such as cats.

A lid also offers the advantage that the air between the water surface and the lid usually stays warm. Since betta fish are labyrinth fish and therefore not only take in oxygen through their gills, but also gasp for atmospheric air through their mouths at the water surface, this air should not be much colder than the tank water. This prevents the betta fish from being exposed to excessive temperature fluctuations. The lid should of course allow air exchange so that the air quality is good.

Betta fish enjoy a densely planted home and like to swim through and around the plants. Plants can also serve as hiding places. Furthermore, it is a good idea to offer a betta fish at least one retreat, for example in the form of a cave or a tube.

Small fish beds are also very popular. These are ideally placed on a wall of the tank near the water surface. Many fish like to rest in such "beds".

It is often advised to choose a dark substrate for the betta fish tank. However, experience shows that it makes no difference whether the substrate is light or dark. Either is fine. However, it should not be reflective, but dull.

Betta fish like lots of plants in their tank, but they should also have enough space to swim. The plants should not have any sharp edges - not even on the leaves - so that the betta fish does not injure itself on them. Especially long-finned fish should live in a tank that is not too heavily planted, so that they do not have to "squeeze" through the plants too much with their large fins but have enough space to reach everywhere with their fins.

If you use a water filter, you should make sure that it does not suck in the fins and that the betta fish cannot get caught in it. Therefore, many mechanical filters are rather unsuitable, because many of them have too large suction openings that can suck in the fins. For this reason, smaller, air-driven filters are usually more suitable.

To keep the water pleasantly warm, small regulating heaters that can be immersed in the water are a good idea, especially in the cooler months.

Betta fish prefer rather dark places and like to stay in the shade of plants and caves, but sufficient lighting should be provided for the plants. Aquarium lamps are well suited for this purpose.

© *Sirawit Seengam*

Water

Betta fish are warm water fish. The ideal water temperature in the tank should be between 22°C and 32°C (approx. between 70°F and 89°F). Most keepers have the best experiences with a water temperature of about 24°C (75°F).

Some fish keepers change their water by about 10% daily. However, it is also possible to do a "big" water change only once a week and change about 50% of the water. This depends on the individual conditions of the tank. Attention should also be paid to how the tank looks and how the fish behaves. Water changes should also be carried out if water values deteriorate.

Water changes reduce the risk of disease and improve the well-being of the Betta fish. Furthermore, this will keep ammonia, nitrate and nitrite to a minimum.

The pH level of the water should be between 6.0 and 8.0.

The total hardness of the water should be between 6 °e/°Clark and 19 °e/°Clark (*between 90°aH/ppm and 270°aH/ppm*). Softer water is therefore better than hard water.

The carbonate hardness should be less than 5 °e/°Clark (*less than 70 °aH/ppm*).

Nitrate is converted into nitrite. The nitrite level (NO2) should always be zero; if it rises, a water change should be carried out. At a nitrite level of more than 0.5 mg per litre (*0.5 ppm*) it becomes toxic for the fish!

The nitrate level (NO3) should also be kept low. It should not exceed 20 mg per litre (*20 ppm*). If it rises above this, a water change should also be carried out. It becomes toxic at a value of over 35 mg per litre (*35 ppm*)!

The subject of water filters is a frequent topic of dispute in the betta fish community. Many keepers use a water filter, but some also run completely technic-free tanks with success and good water values. I advise using a small water filter. With a filter, the water values are usually kept more stable. Furthermore, "good" bacteria settle in the water filter. These are important for the metabolic cycle and are not harmful. The pipe should be located just below the water surface so that the surface moves. Since betta fish also live in rivers and canals, they can cope with a low current.

You should also refrain from cleaning the water filter too meticulously, as you run the risk of eliminating all the "good" bacteria. If no diseases occur, it is usually sufficient to clean the filter only roughly every few months.

© 13683717

Plants

The fish tank should definitely be equipped with some plants; how many plants are chosen and what size they are depends on the individual tank. Plants are important to maintain the balance of the tank. In addition, the betta fish should have enough plants to hide behind and to seek out shady spots.

However, the tank should not be crammed with too many plants so that the fish still has enough room to swim and so that it does not have to squeeze through the plants with its sometimes large fins.

For betta fish tanks, it is advisable to use fast-growing and herbaceous plants. A good mixture of floating plants and ground covers is also a good idea.

Plants such as water lettuce (Pistia stratiotes), water fern, crypt (water trumpet), Java moss (Vesicularia dubyana), Java fern (Microsorum pteropus), Vallisneria or smooth frogbit (Limnobium laevigatum) are particularly suitable. In addition, most betta fish are very happy to accept large Anubias leaves to rest on!

Water lettuce has smooth leaves and is mainly found in tropical waters. Although it is very temperature-resistant, it depends on sufficient light irradiation.

Water fern is also very temperature-resistant but does not need as much light as water lettuce. The large water fern is native to the American continent. The plant grows very densely; therefore, it may need to be shortened to ensure that the bottom of the tank is not completely dark.

Crypt (water trumpet) grow medium high. There are a few different species - Albida or Wendtii are particularly suitable, for example. Albidas have narrow, green leaves and grow slowly. Wendtiis also have green leaves, but they are wider than the leaves of the Albida. Both are very easy to care for and are not very demanding.

Java moss attaches itself to the fixtures in the tank over time. These include mainly stones and roots, on which java moss likes to grow. It does not have high demands and is a very low-maintenance plant.

Vallisneria plants cover the surface of the water well, grow quickly and can also be shortened easily. They are therefore very adaptable.

Smooth frogbit feels comfortable at a temperature between 20 and a maximum of 29 °C (*approx. between 68 and 84°F*). It is native to tropical areas in America and has even smoother leaves than water lettuce. Smooth frogbit grows very quickly but can easily be shortened.

© *Christy Hammer*

Cycling Phase

The cycling phase is very important for every betta fish tank. Unfortunately, inexperienced fish owners often make the mistake of preparing the tank and then immediately putting the fish into the tank. However, keeping betta fish needs to be well thought out and it takes a few weeks to get the tank ready.

During the cycling phase, important bacteria build up in the tank, creating a natural balance in the new fish home.

Once you have a clean tank, the substrate has been rinsed off and filled in and the water has been added, the aquatic plants can be added on the same day or the next. Before the betta fish can move in, the water values must first settle. The cycling phase varies in length, but usually lasts between three and six weeks.

The water values should be checked and documented regularly. It can happen that the aquatic plants weaken somewhat or even die off, as the nutrient balance is not yet at its optimum during the cycling phase.

This is okay - the plants should not be replaced or anything else changed during the cycling phase. If necessary, new plants can be added after the cycling phase. There is no need to change the water during the cycling phase either.

The optimal water values can be found in the chapter "Water". During the cycling phase there will be a so-called nitrite peak. The nitrite value will rise and then reach a peak. Exactly when this happens is very individual and depends on the size of the tank, the planting etc.

The nitrite peak often occurs between the first and third week and usually lasts a few days. After that, the nitrite value will drop again. When the optimal water values are reached, the betta fish can move into its new home.

Unfortunately, it is sometimes claimed that the cycling phase is not necessary for betta fish, as nitrite does not harm them. This is not correct. Nitrite is also harmful to betta fish. It enters the bloodstream of the fish and prevents the smooth transport of oxygen - it doesn't matter if it is taken in by the gills or the labyrinth organ.

Nitrite can trigger diseases and even kill the fish if the level is too high. It is therefore always advisable to let the tank cycle first, wait for the nitrite peak and only let the fish move in when the nitrite level has dropped to zero again.

© Josh Clifford

Socialisation

I advise against keeping a betta fish in a social group - regardless of whether it is with other betta fish or with other fish species.

The betta splendens must absolutely live in single keeping. With wild types, opinions differ - there are breeders and keepers who successfully keep wild types together in one tank. Whether this is successful, however, is a very individual question. Those fish are also aggressive and insist on having their own territory. Especially a beginner is better advised to keep each betta fish in its own tank.

It does not always have to come to fights with maiming or fatality - even if this does not happen, the betta fish can be very stressed by its company. This is not always apparent. Many betta fish sooner or later bow to their fate, as they cannot escape the situation. However, this stresses the fish very much, weakens the immune system, promotes diseases and in the worst case scenario shortens the life of the fish. Keeping a harem (=one male with several females) is also not recommended, even if this is still often suggested - just as little as a pure "female community".

If you keep betta fish together with long-finned guppies, for example, you run the risk that the betta fish will think the guppy is a rival and fight it. The problem with fish like danios is that they are very lively and active, which can cause stress to the betta fish.

Neon wrasses are also too lively and bustling for a betta fish, which feels stressed by this. Some other fish species nibble and gnaw on the betta fish's tail fins. The list could be continued endlessly - so socialisation is extremely difficult and often impossible.

As this is a book for beginners, I advise keeping betta fish strictly solitary. Betta fish do not need too much space or too large a tank - so you can get more tanks relatively easily if you want to keep more than one fish.

However, it is no problem to keep a betta fish together with snails or shrimps. Especially with shrimps, however, it is important to bear in mind that the betta fish likes to eat them sometimes - and that the shrimps turn out to be expensive live food in the end.

If you want to keep snails together with the betta fish, post horn snails or racing snails are particularly suitable. Snails also have the advantage that they keep the tank clean and save the owner a lot of work.

© Cuong Nguyen

BETTA SPLENDENS FOR BEGINNERS

Diet

Betta fish are strict carnivores. Therefore, they cannot digest plant food and are dependent on animal proteins. For this reason, the diet of a betta fish must be well thought out.

You can choose between fresh food, industrial dry food or a combination of both.

If you want to give your betta fish (also) industrially processed dry food, you must pay close attention to the composition of the food. Many types of food contain a high proportion of vegetable components or general fillers, as these are naturally cheaper to produce.

However, this does your betta fish no favours, as it will not be able to use the vegetable components anyway. For this reason, it is important that the food contains as much animal food as possible.

Vegetable components are not only excreted without being utilised but can also cause health problems. If the proportion of vegetable components is too high, this can lead to constipation, general digestive problems and discomfort. For this reason, industrially produced food should consist of at least 45% animal protein. Granules with a proportion of more than 55% are hard to find and also not necessary. There are no granules or pellets without any vegetable components, as these act as a bonding agent or "glue" and hold the individual components together.

Fresh animal protein should also not be missing when feeding granules. Therefore, it is recommended to either feed only fresh food (live and/or dead) or to choose a combination of both untreated and industrially produced food.

Live food can include, for example, mosquito larvae, water fleas, blackworms, artemia/fairy shrimp/brine shrimp, tubifex and enchytrae.

Mosquito larvae and artemia, for example, can also be fed dead, as can cyclops.

If you want to offer frozen food, it must be fed immediately after thawing. Only as much food should be thawed as is needed for one feeding. This can be easily portioned with the help of a sharp knife. During thawing, the food begins to rot and must therefore be consumed quickly. The thawing process is important, however, as frozen food should not be put into the tank frozen, as this is simply too cold for the betta fish - a warm water fish. Frozen food can lead to digestive problems and further diseases.

Furthermore, frozen food should be rinsed well. The water that is produced during the thawing process should not be added to the tank but poured away. The easiest way to do this is to use a fine sieve. The water will most likely contain droppings and other dead body parts - these should not enter the betta fish's tank.

How often the betta fish is fed should be determined individually. Under no circumstances should the fish become too fat, as obesity can also lead to further diseases in fish - but of course it should not be too thin either. Obesity does indeed often occur in fish and is a very common cause of death, as some keepers "mean too well with their fish". The betta fish does not usually separate and regulate its food but eats what is put in front of it. Obesity can lead to further diseases, the fish can suffer from digestive problems, the organs (especially the liver) can become fatty etc.

Many owners feed their betta fish once a day. Ideally, feeding should always take place at the same time. Some keepers also feed their betta fish twice a day, usually in the morning and evening, and give them smaller amounts each time. Both is fine.

Betta fish can even fast for one or two days without suffering. Therefore, many owners set aside one fasting day per week. However, this is not necessary. But if you go away for the weekend (Friday to Sunday), the betta fish can go without feeding on Saturday without anyone having to come home and feed the fish.

If live food is fed, about five small animals are usually enough. However, this also depends on the type of animal being fed. Mosquito larvae, for example, contain a lot of water (black mosquito larvae 81%, red mosquito larvae 87% and white mosquito larvae 90%) and not too much fat, so even around ten mosquito larvae can be offered per day.

Artemia, on the other hand, contain a lot of fat (approx. 7%) and should therefore not be offered too often. Water fleas/daphnia contain a high proportion of dietary fibre, extremely little fat and are therefore good for intestinal cleansing. Cyclops also have a high fibre content.

If granules are fed, a pinch is sufficient. The granules should not float around in the water for long but be eaten by the betta fish within a few minutes. For this reason, it is advisable to feed only small amounts of granules.

© *Cuong Nguyen*

15 Common Diseases

1. Anchor worms

Normally, anchor worms are visible to the naked eye as they are relatively large and attach themselves to the body and fins. They are dark in colour - usually grey - and the betta fish usually rubs itself against the tank accessories to relieve the itching caused by the anchor worms. They are often introduced into the fish tank via live food but are less common than most of the other worm species that can affect a betta fish.

2. Tapeworms

Tapeworm infestations in betta fish are similar to those in humans. The tapeworm nests in the betta fish's intestine and usually causes a reduced appetite, weight loss, but also a discolouration of the fish's body. Tapeworms belong to the nematodes and can grow very long - in betta fish they sometimes even reach several centimetres in length. Tapeworms are usually transmitted to the betta fish through live food.

3. Dropsy

Dropsy is usually caused by other diseases - mainly tumours, poor kidney function or kidney failure, or even a bacterial infection. Dropsy is usually easy to recognise because the abdomen looks bloated and the scales stick out. Treatment is difficult, because dropsy is already the final stage, in which the organs usually no longer function well or have already given up. The entire body of the fish fills with water and the scales protrude from the body. It may be possible to treat the disease with some antibiotics, which an expert veterinarian can prescribe, but the chances are rather poor in most cases.

4. Columnaris

Columnaris is a very serious disease in betta fish. It is an aggressive bacterial infestation (Myxobacteria / Flexibacter). Many bacterial diseases are triggered by a weakened immune system, which in turn is usually due to too much stress (socialisation, poor water values, too cold water etc.). The treatment of columnaris is difficult and antibacterial medication is necessary, which can be prescribed by a vet. Unfortunately, however, columnaris often leads to the death of the animal. The disease causes a white coating to form on the skin very quickly, which usually covers the entire body within a few hours and can also cause bloodshot areas on the body. In order to prevent the death of the animal, action must be taken very quickly, as this often occurs after only one day.

5. Threadworms

Threadworms are often difficult to detect as they are very small and usually found in the animal's faeces. Symptoms include rapid weight loss of the betta fish, even when they are eating their food and not suffering from loss of appetite.

6. Fish tuberculosis

Fish tuberculosis is a bacterial infection. The bacteria are of the genus Mycobacterium. The symptoms are very varied and range from weight loss/lack of appetite, goggle eyes and swimming problems to inflammation of the skin or scales and their darkening colouration.

7. Fin rot

Fin rot is relatively easy to recognise as the fins are mangled and frayed. Sometimes the fins are also inflamed or bleed a little. The ability to swim can deteriorate for some fish due to fin rot and they can appear apathetic. Usually the fish clamps its fins, but it does not chafe like a worm infestation. The causes of fin rot are usually due to a weak immune system - in addition, poor housing conditions such as poor water quality, lack of a varied diet and stressful situations (e.g., group housing) increase susceptibility to fin rot and other diseases. Fin rot is caused by the bacteria Aeromonas and Pseudomonas. In case of an infestation, the betta fish should be treated in a quarantine box against bacterial infections with appropriate medication. A large water change should be carried out in the tank itself.

8. Googly eyes / goggle eyes

Googly eyes are usually caused by a bacterial infection and are easy to recognise because the eyes swell up and look milky or whitish. This can also affect only one of the two eyes. Often, googly eyes are caused by a small injury to the eye that allows bacteria to enter the wound and inflame the eye. However, this is not always the case. The condition is usually easily treatable and can be alleviated with appropriate medication. Sometimes it is sufficient to keep the betta fish in a quarantine box for one to two weeks, change the water there daily and, if necessary, give salt baths. It is a good idea to lower the water temperature slightly (to about 20°C) for the duration of the disease, as the bacteria are less active in slightly colder water.

9. Skin worms

Skin worms are usually larger than gill worms and measure about 0.3 to 0.5 millimetres. They nest on the scales of the fish and are often visible to the naked eye, as part of the worm usually protrudes from the scales. A fish infested with skin worms will often rub itself against objects in the tank to get rid of the worms.

10. Ichthyophthirius (ICH; white spot disease)

ICH occurs not only in betta fish, but in many ornamental fish species. A betta fish that has ICH will have white spots on the body, especially on the fins and gills. Affected fish also often appear apathetic. Betta fish often fall ill with this disease when they are exposed to great stress and their immune system has been weakened as a result. They then usually try to remove the parasites by rubbing against plants and other objects. The white spots on the fish body are larger in ICH than the spots in Oodinium.

11. Gill worms

As the name suggests, gill worms nest in the gills of a fish and also lay their eggs there. This parasite is about 0.1 to 0.3 millimetres long and poses a great danger to the fish. The gills of the infected fish become red and sometimes even bleed.

12 Oodinium (velvet disease)

Oodinium is also mainly triggered when the betta fish is exposed to severe stress and its immune system weakens as a result. At the beginning, the disease is usually asymptomatic and can therefore only be recognised at an advanced stage. Similar to ICH, the betta fish scrub their bodies on objects in the tank to eliminate the parasites. At this stage, the disease may not even be visible. Over time, white and/or golden spots will form on the body. However, these are much smaller than the spots in ICH.

13. Pocket inflammation

If a betta fish suffers from a pocket infection, the scales partially protrude from the body. In some cases, reddened areas can also be seen on the body. In contrast to dropsy, however, the entire body is not swollen, but the inflammation usually occurs in the area of the neck, the head and/or the flanks. A common cause of psoriasis is minor injuries that allow bacteria to enter the body and cause water to be deposited in the body. This causes the scales to stick out and the affected area to become swollen.

14. Tumours

Even with the best and most species-appropriate husbandry, tumours can develop. As in humans, tumours in betta fish can be benign or malignant. Many betta fish live a long and happy life even with a tumour. Unfortunately, nothing can be done against malignant tumours, as an operation and corresponding removal of the tumour is not an option for the small betta fish. A tumour can be recognised by the formation of a small, hard spot on the scale layer - or a tumour node.

15. Obesity

Overweight is unfortunately common in fish, including the betta fish. The betta fish does not usually regulate its diet itself but eats whatever is provided by humans. Therefore, the owner is responsible for regulating the diet and watching the weight of the fish. Obesity can not only lead to digestive problems but can also cause the organs - especially the liver - to become fatty and lead to failure of these organs.

For initial care, it is a good idea to always have a food-safe quarantine box in the house. In this box, the fish can be treated more specifically. The box should hold about two to five litres and have a lid with holes. The holes can of course also be made in the lid by hand. The quarantine box can and should not have a substrate, plants, etc.

The water in the quarantine box is changed daily and the bottom and the edges are briefly wiped with a sponge to remove excess bacteria. In the quarantine box, the betta fish can be better observed in order to follow the course of the disease. Furthermore, it is easier to administer medication in the box. The water level in the box should be low so that the betta fish can always easily reach the water surface to gasp for air.

Salt baths can also be carried out well in a small quarantine box (not in the tank!). It is important that the salt does not contain iodine! Conventional dishwasher salt is also suitable for a salt bath. For a salt bath, add about two to three teaspoons of salt to about twenty litres of water. Of course, this depends on the size of the quarantine box. For example, if the box holds five litres of water, one teaspoon of salt can be added to the water.

The salt stimulates the mucous membrane of the fish and works particularly well for inflammations, small injuries or diseases of the fins. Because the salt dries out the skin, the betta fish increases the production of mucus. This eliminates bacteria and parasites.

Indian almond leaves can also help against inflammations, as they have an antibacterial effect. For this purpose, one litre of boiling water is added to one Indian almond leaf, which in turn produces a kind of tea.

However, you should wait a few hours to let the brew steep properly. 100 to 200 millilitres of this tea can then be added to the fish tank; it should not be more. Alternatively, the leaf can be added directly to the tank. It is normal that the water then often takes on a slightly brownish colour.

In case of doubt and in case of acute illness, always consult a competent veterinarian.

© *Holger Grybsch*

Legal Notice

Author: Alina Daria Djavidrad

Contact: Wiesenstr. 6, 45964 Gladbeck, Germany

© 2021 Alina Daria Djavidrad

1st edition (2021)

© Yan Cabrera

Space for Notes

Printed in Great Britain
by Amazon